TENSHIN-EN

The Garden of the Heart of Heaven

TENSHIN-EN

The Garden of the Heart of Heaven

Julie Moir Messervy
with contributions by Jan Fontein
and Kinsaku Nakane

Museum of Fine Arts, Boston

Copyright ©1993
Museum of Fine Arts, Boston

ISBN 0-878476-371-2
Library of Congress catalogue card no.
93-077922

Designed and typeset in Monotype Bembo
 by Janet O'Donoghue
Edited by Cynthia Purvis
Photography by the Department of
 Photographic Services, Museum of Fine Arts,
 Boston, except pages 5, 12, and 15.
Calligraphy by Kaji Aso

Frontispiece:

Six hundred azaleas of mixed colors and varieties billow forth at the bases of rocks and trees. Here, the red 'Hinocrimson' and 'Hinodegiri' varieties combine with the double-white bloom of 'Polar Bear' to suggest miniature hills and valleys among the soft mosses. The Japanese maple (Acer palmatum), *a signature plant of a Japanese garden, has a horizontal branching structure and brilliant scarlet foliage in autumn.*

On the Cover:

Looking across the Tortoise Island (kamejima), *the white, drooping panicles of andromeda* (Pieris japonica) *contrast with the soft reds, whites, and pinks of azaleas. Haircap mosses* (Polytrichum commune) *and Japanese junipers* (Juniperus procumbens Nana) *drape the stones, all local granites selected for their size, shape, and striations.*

TENSHIN-EN, THE JAPANESE GARDEN on the grounds of the Museum of Fine Arts, Boston—the repository of one of the world's finest collections of Asian Art—was built to commemorate the achievements of Okakura Kakuzō, who served the Museum as the second curator of its Department of Asiatic Art. I would like to express my most sincere gratitude to Mr. Yōsōji Kobayashi, chairman of the board of the Nippon Television Network Corporation, whose generosity made the garden a realized dream. I would also like to commend and offer my appreciation to the numerous persons whose combined efforts made possible the publication of this brochure, which, I am confident, will contribute toward introducing the essence of Japanese culture and spirit to the more than eight hundred thousand visitors the Museum welcomes annually from around the world.

In 1990, the Museum celebrated the first centenary of its Department of Asiatic Art. In the same year, the Kubota Corporation celebrated the first centenary of its foundation by Gonshirō Kubota. Centered around such agricultural equipment as tractors, and expanding into wide-ranging, diverse fields, the company has gone on to develop products that support the foundation of human life. In recent years, the company has emphasized research and development to incorporate leading-edge technology in a positive effort to foresee the products that will meet the evolving needs of the future. And because we at Kubota have also been focusing attention on participation in cultural activities, we consider ourselves exceptionally fortunate to have had the opportunity to contribute toward making this publication a reality.

Shigekazu Mino
President, Kubota Corporation

FOREWORD

THE MUSEUM OF FINE ARTS, BOSTON, opened Tenshin-en, the Garden of the Heart of Heaven, on October 24, 1988, as an exciting addition to its world-renowned Asiatic collection. The garden provides a place of beauty and serenity for Museum visitors to sit quietly and contemplate the spiritual and aesthetic composition of this traditional Japanese art form. Designed by Professor Kinsaku Nakane of Kyoto and built by a team of Japanese and American craftsmen, the garden was a generous gift of the Nippon Television Network Corporation, Mr. Yōsōji Kobayashi, chairman of the board. This lovely book, which tells the history and design of the building of Tenshin-en, is the thoughtful gift of another Japanese company, the Kubota Corporation.

The garden and the book are both new examples of the Museum's friendly relations with Japan and the Japanese people, and of the cultural exchange between Boston and Japan, which now has extended over a period of more than a hundred years.

Alan Shestack
Director, Museum of Fine Arts, Boston

THE JAPANESE GARDEN AT THE MUSEUM OF FINE ARTS, BOSTON, is named after Okakura Kakuzō, former curator of the Museum's Department of Asiatic Art. The garden includes stone lanterns and a pagoda from the Museum's collection that were cherished by Okakura, as well as items brought from Japan when the garden was built.

Tenshin-en covers an area of approximately 10,000 square feet. The entrance to the garden is a *bukemon* medieval-style gate. Specially trained carpenters (*miya daiku*) traveled to Boston from Kyoto, Japan, to build this gate. The entire garden is surrounded by a *tsuijibei*-style traditional garden wall.

Tenshin-en embodies the *karesansui* garden, one of the traditional Japanese garden forms. The goal of a *karesansui* garden is to suggest magnificent scenes of nature by forming the shapes of various landscape elements such as waterfalls, mountains, islands, and ocean. The shore represented in the Boston garden is based on an impression of the beautiful New England coastline found near the city. The main emphasis has been placed on the summit of the waterfall (*takiguchi*). On a mound that suggests a solemn mountain, a number of stones are arranged to represent the *takiguchi*. The water falls from the summit into a pond and then flows out into the sea around islands of various sizes. Several mountains form descending slopes from the high mountain where the *takiguchi* is located, while elegant natural scenery can be seen in the background beyond the ocean. Thus, the design of this garden expresses the vastness of nature in miniature, within a strictly limited space.

The *karesansui* garden style as represented by Tenshin-en derives from Zen philosophy, which was brought to Japan from China during the early medieval era of Japanese history (late twelfth to early

THE JAPANESE GARDEN, TENSHIN-EN

Kinsaku Nakane

Under Professor Nakane's watchful eye, 178 boulders were positioned in harmony, as if connected by a single thread.

thirteenth centuries). The intention of this art is to depict shapes of physical entities by representation or by implication, based on the Zen view of the Universe and Nature. In Tenshin-en, one may see and hear a cascade of water tumbling from the *takiguchi*, and calm sea waves in the white sand of the garden. The natural stones were gathered from around Boston. The trees and plants include some from Japan as well as those indigenous to New England.

Among the various styles of Japanese gardens, the *karesansui* garden requires the highest degree of sensitivity and artistic skill. The artist must design the scenery around the summit of the waterfall in such a manner as to imply the falling of water without actually using water itself: the design must strongly represent and imply, dynamically and statically, a rapid flow gushing against rocks as well as a sea full of water.

One of the important points of *karesansui* garden building is the treatment of stones. The designer must have an extremely keen sense of artistry in arranging the rocks and stones. Dozens, or even hundreds, of stones must be positioned in harmony as if they are all connected by a single invisible thread. Single stones or groups of stones must be set at exactly the spots that imply the movement of flowing water, its rush, and lethargy. Even one single rock placed out of synchronization may greatly affect the result. The *takiguchi*, islands, sea, coastline, and scattered floating stones of Tenshin-en have all been designed and arranged with these functions fully taken into consideration. The curve of the line of the mountains here also plays an important role, together with the plants and trees.

Looking across a mossy bank to the crushed granite gravel sea, the Tortoise Island (kame-jima) is defined by two of three curved granite bridges: its head, the large stone to the left of the middle bridge; its tail, the flat stone at the terminus of the bridge on the left; its flipper, the large curved stone at the center of the island, and its feet to either side of the flipper. Tortoise Islands are a Taoist symbol of longevity, and appear often in traditonal Japanese gardens.

Kinsaku Nakane is president of Osaka University of the Arts and president of the Nakane Garden Research and Construction Corporation in Kyoto, Japan.

This Korean lantern of the Chosŏn period (sixteenth to seventeenth centuries) was originally located in the Museum's courtyard. The roof and the base are of different origins. Its stark architectural form gives emphasis to the corner where the massive façade of the West Wing joins the Evans Wing.

THE JAPANESE GARDEN OF THE MUSEUM OF FINE ARTS has a history as long as that of the building itself. In 1909 when the Museum moved from Copley Square to Guy Lowell's new building on The Fenway, the galleries housing the Museum's great collection of Japanese painting and sculpture were designed around an interior Japanese garden. In an environment enhanced by wooden columns and brackets in Japanese style, this ground-floor garden was best viewed from the balustrade of the second floor, decorated with Japanese wood carvings. The garden had Japanese trees and shrubs, rocks, a granite pagoda and lantern, and a pond. A paucity of written or visual documentation leaves unanswered the question to what extent the distinguished Japanese curator Okakura Kakuzō, author of *The Book of Tea*, had a hand in its creation. What little evidence there is suggests that the Japanese garden, as we knew it during the sixties and seventies, was the result of drastic modification of the original design. At one time the wide open area behind the garden was walled in to create additional storage space. The sparse daylight admitted through the discolored corrugated Plexiglas of the skylight was unable to sustain the life of the trees and shrubs. Consequently, the frequent introduction of new plant material may well have changed much of the garden's original appearance.

By far the most dramatic change was the result of an accident, a near disaster. During the late fifties the goldfish pond suddenly sprang a leak, inundating the basement underneath where Nō costumes were stored. Only the timely and energetic intervention by members of the Ladies Committee, led by Frannie (Weeks) Lawrence, prevented a disaster.

Subsequently, the pond was filled with sand and gravel, transforming the garden into one of the so-called "dry landscape" (*karesansui*) type. While many still cherish fond memories of the old garden, it was, in its final years, more of a monument to Boston's century-long fascination with

The original garden, located in the Japanese galleries, before their renovation.

The garden is named in honor of one of the first curators of the Department of Asiatic Art — Okakura Kakuzō, also known as Okakura Tenshin, the author of The Book of Tea.

things Japanese than a representative example of Japanese garden architecture.

When plans were made for the renovation of the galleries and for the introduction of climate control to safeguard the collection against the extremes of Boston's weather, the interests of conservation as well as practical considerations demanded the removal of the garden to an outdoor location. By eliminating the interior garden and filling in the second floor, the Museum gained two large new galleries for the display of Japanese art. But acquiring additional space was not our only objective. The interior garden was what Kōichi Kawana in his essay, "The Challenge of Building a Japanese Garden in the United States," calls a "Japanese Garden." The Museum of Fine Arts, with the finest collection of Japanese art in the Western world, deserved a Japanese garden without quotation marks, a garden that could be appreciated by a new generation of visitors, many of whom have seen with their own eyes the great classical gardens of Japan.

It was at this stage of planning, in May 1978, that the Government of Japan, under the leadership of Premier Takeo Fukuda, made the unprecedented offer to provide the funds for the renovation of the Japanese galleries. As it was this renovation that necessitated the relocation of the garden, it seemed only logical to seek Japanese support for the construction of a new garden as well.

Mr. Yōsōji Kobayashi, then president of the Nippon Television Network Corporation, a staunch friend of the Museum with whom we were already working on an exhibition of the Museum's treasures in Japan, was an obvious choice. Anyone who has visited the Azumaya, Mr. Kobayashi's tea house and garden in the heart of Tokyo, will be convinced of his unswerving commitment to perpetuating the traditions of the Tea Ceremony and its natural environment, the Japanese garden. Surrounded on all sides by the towering skyscrapers of downtown Tokyo, the Azumaya is a refuge from the bustling corporate world outside. With the modesty so often found in persons of broad vision, Mr. Kobayashi gives much of the credit for the preservation of the

Tokyo landmark to the IBM Corporation, which long ago had ceded the land to NTV. With his generous gift of a Japanese garden to the Boston Museum, Mr. Kobayashi wished to reciprocate the goodwill gesture of an American company that had enabled him to create the garden of the Azumaya in Tokyo.

While the renovation of the galleries proceeded according to plan and their reopening was celebrated on November 1, 1982, much thought was given to a possible site for the new garden. Originally many considered proximity to the Department of Asiatic Art a priority. Even the option of a roof garden was carefully considered. However, a survey of roof gardens in Japan, including Nagare Masayuki's garden on top of the Tokyo Tenri Kaikan, revealed the limitations and drawbacks of this option; it was, therefore, soon discarded. When the rerouting of vehicle access to the loading dock of the Museum, as a result of the construction of I.M. Pei's West Wing, precluded the selection of a site on the west side of the Asiatic Wing, the focus shifted to the Museum's western courtyard. Particularly useful to an assessment of the design problems posed by this site was a semester-long seminar for students of the Harvard School of Design, directed by the late Cherrie Kluesing. This in-depth study of the potential of the site confirmed the fears of many participants that the Western architecture enclosing the courtyard would impinge upon the design of a Japanese garden. In the end, however, other, largely practical considerations dictated the final choice of a site. The logistical problems of constructing a garden in an enclosed area and the additional costs it would entail, combined with the prospect of having to reroute existing underground ductwork, led to a reopening of the search for an alternative site.

Moreover, further progress in the Museum's overall long-range planning made all involved in the process aware of the risks of constructing a garden in an area that future generations might wish to convert to other Museum use. All of these seemingly negative considerations contributed to a positive result. The final choice of a site to the north of the Museum's West Wing met all of the criteria and offered some other advantages as well. Constructed in an area least likely to be affected by future expansion, the garden could be viewed from both levels of the Museum, while the trees planted along The Fenway would provide the suitable backdrop that the Japanese call "borrowed scenery." Seen from The Fenway, the garden's plain walls would blend harmoniously with the stark simplicity of the north façade of I.M. Pei's West Wing.

Of course, just as important as the search for funds and the search for a site was the choice of an architect to build the right Japanese garden for us. Although I initially approached this task with some trepidation, it turned out to be one of the most rewarding duties of my directorship of the Museum.

My own initiation in the appreciation of modern Japanese garden architecture had occurred in the fall of 1954 during my first visit to Kyoto as a student. By a fortunate coincidence the great collector and patron of the arts, Hosokawa Moritatsu, had taken a personal interest in my education in things Japanese. It was he who opened my eyes to the genius of the great Japanese garden architect of the Meiji era, Ogawa Jihei, whose creations include the residence of the Hosokawa family near the Nanzenji temple in Kyoto. A year of study under the enlightened guidance of the tea master Yabunouchi Shōchi introduced me to the esthetics of the Tea Ceremony, the tea house and its natural habitat, the garden. While these experiences enriched my sojourn in Japan and deepened my interest in Japanese culture, I had no inkling how useful they would be later in my life.

Of course, participating in tea ceremonies in ancient shrines and admiring their great gardens is something quite different from viewing contemporary gardens for the purpose of selecting an architect. In the course of frequent trips to Japan I visited many gardens and nurseries, talking to monks and gardeners, looking for trees and shrubs that would be hardy enough to survive the rigors of the Boston climate. I even acquired from a Japanese dealer a Korean stone lantern of the Chosŏn period (sixteenth to seventeenth centuries) after having seen a similar lantern in Ogawa Jihei's beautiful garden of the Sumito-mo family residence in Kyoto.

On another occasion, when I visited the botanical garden of the University of Hokkaido, I discovered a pendulous variety of the Katsura tree (*Cercidiphyllum magnificum var. pendulum*). When such a tree turned up shortly afterward at an auction of rare plants at the Arnold Arboretum it was acquired for the Muse-um. It stayed in the nursery of the Arboretum until the garden would be ready to receive it. In all this I received much valuable advice and constant encour-agement from the late Paul Bernat, whose genuine appreciation of Japanese gardens, whose connoisseur's eye for trees and shrubs, and whose deep person-al interest in this project were a constant source of moral support and an inspi-ration to me.

After receiving some recommendations made by Mr. Kobayashi and his staff, Paul Bernat, accompanied by his wife Helen, and I traveled to Japan for an extended tour of contemporary Japanese gardens. My first excursion in Tokyo led me to the stone garden of the Konishi Sake Brewery, created by Fukaya

Great benefactors Paul and Helen Bernat in Japan. Paul Bernat helped select the architect of the garden and chose many of the focal trees and shrubs.

Kōki. In the course of a conversation with the president of the brewery, he drew my attention to Kōjiro Yū-ichirō's book, *Famous Contemporary Gardens* (Genzai no Mei-en, Tokyo: Kodansha, 1980), in which his garden figures prominently. That same day I got a copy of that book, which was to serve as our guide in the days ahead. Aided by its superb illustrations, we were able to nar-row our search down to nine architects, all of whom seemed promising in differ-ent ways.

Mindful of our specific mission, but keeping an open mind as to the type of garden we should look for, we began our search paying special attention to gardens that had been designed for Western-style buildings. Among these were the gardens of the Keio Plaza Hotel and the headquarters of the Hino Motor Company, both designed by Fukaya Kōki. After viewing a number of these gardens, we began to realize that their principal purpose seemed to be to provide a typically Japanese accent to buildings in a rather bland, Western architectural style.

Naturally, we paid special attention to gardens of museums. Most of the many museums in Japan, public as well as private, that have been built during the last thirty years, have been given their own garden. These represent a wide range of types, from the classic Zen simplicity of rocks and gravel to modern stone abstractions, from small courtyard miniature *tsubo niwa* ("jar gardens") to the vast, undulating gardens of the MOA museum at Atami. Set against a borrowed landscape of old pine trees, the sparse rock and moss garden of the Gyokudō Art Museum at Oume near Tokyo seemed most effective. It offered an interesting contrast to the densely planted garden of the Nihon Geijutsu-in Kaikan, both designed by Nakajima Ken.

What came to us as a real surprise was the state of neglect in which we found several of the privately owned contemporary gardens. Accustomed to the meticulously manicured classical gardens of Kyoto, we were astonished to find some gardens with waterfalls and streams poorly maintained, their ductwork in disrepair, their trees overgrown and shapeless. In one case our persistence in trying to locate a little-known private garden off the beaten track led to the discovery that its original design by a prominent architect had been irretrievably spoiled by the recent excavation of a swimming pool. It made us realize that great contemporary gardens, before they reach the age of maturity and achieve official recognition as spots of scenic beauty, may suffer periods of decline and neglect, a danger for which the high cost of garden maintenance is at least in part to blame. All this gave us cause to think of the long-range viability of our own project.

In Kyoto we could not resist the pleasure of visiting several of Ogawa Jihei's masterpieces, such as the Nomura Garden, the Sumitomo Garden, and the beautiful Tairyū Sansō. But while we were enjoying our visits to the great gardens of the past, we also became acquainted, for the first time, with the gardens designed by Kinsaku Nakane, whom I had previously known only as the author of the small guidebook, *Kyoto Gardens* (Osaka: Hoikusha, 1965) that had often been my guide on my tours of the gardens of the old Imperial city. We first came across his name at the Rakusui-en, an ancient garden that he restored to its original beauty in 1955. His use of a fine type of grass to replace the austere gravel and sand around the rocks, and his effective use of wisteria trellises first made us take notice of his work. We then decided to see some of his other gardens and went to the Taizō-in, a sub-temple of the Myōshinji, known for its treasure, the monochrome Zen painting of a man trying to catch a catfish in a gourd. The Yokō-en garden of that temple with its gently rushing waterfall and beautifully shaped bushes, finished in 1963 after three years of work, is considered by many to be Nakane's masterpiece.

After weeks of traveling, looking at gardens of Buddhist temples, Shintō shrines, museums, inns, and office buildings, there was no discussion; both Paul and I knew whom we wanted to create the Japanese garden for the Museum of Fine Arts.

Just back in Boston to report our findings to the trustees, I received a telephone call from Julie Messervy. She told me that a distinguished Japanese garden architect was about to give a summer course in garden architecture at Harvard University. His name was Kinsaku Nakane. It seemed that at long last the pieces were falling into place. As we saw him at work with his students that summer, building a small private garden in Newton, Massachusetts, we realized that our search had been brought to a successful conclusion.

Before his retirement in 1992, Jan Fontein served as curator of the Department of Asiatic Art, Matsutarō Shōriki Curator for Research, and director of the Museum.

One may be in the midst of a city, and yet feel as if one were far away from the dust and din of civilization.

Okakura Kakuzō, *The Book of Tea*

TENSHIN-EN

Julie Moir Messervy

TENSHIN-EN, THE GARDEN OF THE HEART OF HEAVEN, is one of New England's only Japanese viewing gardens open to the public. Located at the north side of the West Wing of the Museum of Fine Arts, Boston, the garden is named in honor of one of the first curators of the Department of Asiatic Art—Okakura Kakuzō, also known as Okakura Tenshin. It is designed in the *kare-sansui* (*kare* means "dry," *san* means "mountain," and *sui* means "water"), or dry landscape style that harkens back to Zen temple gardens of fifteenth-century Japan, and brings together elements and traditions drawn from Japan, the Museum of Fine Arts, and New England. Each stone, plant, and piece of stone work was chosen from local materials, and combined with stone lanterns, a water basin, and a pagoda from the Museum collection to create a contemplative mood in the midst of a vibrant city. Since its opening, the garden has become a spiritual sanctuary for those who seek it.

The Contemplative Garden

Many Westerners dream of owning a Japanese garden. They imagine returning home to a serene paradise of ancient stones perfectly set in a bed of moss, flanked by rippling waters of a *koi* pond. In this miniature world, they could give voice to their inner thoughts, daydreams, and spirituality.

Few of us will have the space, find the time, or have the funds to create such a sanctuary. How wonderful it is, then, that the Museum of Fine Arts, Boston, has built just such a garden for all to enjoy. Sitting within its walls, closed off from busy Boston traffic and pedestrian onlookers, one feels paradoxically surrounded by, yet removed from urban life. In this curiously transcendent world, the stones feel like ancient souls set with a modern freshness and vigor, remi-

The gently curving stone path (shikiishi) *leads past a water basin* (chōzubachi) *and small stone lantern* (ishidōrō).

A wealth of plant textures—1750 specimens—adorn Tenshin-en's ornamental landscape.

Azaleas are deadheaded and pruned at least twice a year, once immediately after flowering, and once in the late summer, to maintain their shape and size.

niscent of rocky shorelines of the region, yet archetypal in the abstract power of their dry composition.

At first, the energy of the place is overwhelming: 178 rocks, set here and there, both by design and, seemingly, by accident. More than seventy plant species—1750 specimens—adorn the landscape, changing the feeling and form of the garden through the seasons. In early spring, the white-panicled andromeda flowers hang from the shiny green leaves, billowing toward the viewer as a series of ocean waves. Mid-spring into early summer brings a continuous bloom of white, fuchsia, rose, salmon, and pale pink azaleas, hummocking as tiny hills at the feet of tall stones and lanterns. Early summer brings the purple, yellow, and white iris, standing in tall sheaths behind rocks and at the tips of islands. Late summer finds the soft colors of the hosta flowers punctuating the landscape. In fall, the maples, azaleas, and enkianthus turn brilliant hues of red, yellow, and orange to mark the onset of cold, before the snows drape the garden in winter.

Geography of Japan

The timeless quality of Tenshin-en and other well-designed Japanese gardens comes in part from the metaphoric content of their elements. Representing the essence of a natural landscape in miniature, rocks symbolize mountains and islands, and raked gravel suggests the vastness of a sea. It is natural that islands, ponds, and hills should be the basic units of composition of a Japanese garden. Approximately the same size as the state of California, Japan comprises four large islands and more than 3000 smaller ones, with four-fifths of its total land area covered with mountains, many of them volcanic in origin. Habitable space is limited to 145,000 square miles to support both its 120 million population and all its farming activities. More than 60% of the people are crowded into 2.7% of the total land area, living in densely inhabited towns and cities at more than 10,000 people per square mile. Three-quarters of the population lives in dense, low-rise cities, where space, especially for gardens, is at a premium. The ancient capital, Kyoto, is home to most of the famous gardens, many of them built as part of temple or shrine compounds; some of them designed as aristocratic or imperial residences. Most of these are located on the foothills of Kyoto's ring of mountains, and many are open to the public for a small admission fee. Autumn and spring are the best times to visit.

History of the Japanese Garden

The Japanese garden dates to the eighth century. The *Nihon Shoki* (Chronicles of Japan), the second oldest of Japan's histories, mentions garden elements commonly in use, including carp ponds, islands, hillocks, and large stones, all central features in the composition of the traditional Japanese garden as we know it today.

The earliest meaning of *niwa* (garden) was "a place purified for the worship of the gods." According to the indigenous religion, Shintō, certain natural objects—mountains, hills, trees, and stones—house divine spirits. A hiker in the forest might come upon a shrine area spread with white gravel and enclosed in simple bamboo or rope fencing. In the middle might stand a large stone called *iwakura*, which would be bound with ritual rice straw rope, an indication of the presence of *kami*, or spirit guardians. The most famous of these sanctified spaces is the Ise Shrine, on the Ise peninsula jutting into Japan's Inland Sea. For more than a thousand years, this holy site has housed thatched shrine buildings that are fully reconstructed every twenty-one years. An adjacent site stands ready for the new buildings, and when completed, a transferral ceremony is held, and the old ones are then disassembled. Each vacant shrine site, standing in a pristine forest,

This large triangular rock forms the "wing" of the Crane Island. The abstract lines of "water" in the gravel "sea" are most apparent during rainy or cloudy days, or when the textures are emphasized by a thin veneer of snow.

In a Japanese garden, rocks often symbolize mountains and islands, metaphors for that country's particular geographic character.

A heavy, eight-tine rake is used to create the effect of ripples on the crushed granite sea.

suggests the belief in the holiness of natural beauty that is at the heart of the Japanese garden as we know it today.

During the Nara period (710-794), cultural intercourse increased between Japan and T'ang-dynasty China. In its gardens, architecture, legal systems, city design, and even language, Japan began to borrow from its more sophisticated neighbor across the China Sea. The symmetrical design of the garden of the Shishinden, one of the great ceremonial halls of the Kyoto Imperial Palace, suggests this Chinese influence: White gravel—like that found at Ise Shrine— is spread in a courtyard between wooden buildings flanked by a mandarin-orange tree and a cherry tree.

Stroll Gardens

Residential gardens of the Heian period (794-1185) were bright and relaxed gardens that featured large ponds with islands for boating or for viewing. Aristocrats occupied *shinden*-style mansions that faced south, and employed *shōji* (rice-paper screens) and *tatami* (grass mats that covered the floor). Pure Land Buddhism, which offered the hope of salvation and entrance into the Western Paradise after death, exerted a religious influence on garden design. Gardens of the period, whether residential or religious, often attempted to re-create the delights of the paradise offered by Amida Buddha. Ponds with tree-lined shores and rocky islands were the garden ideal, and sophisticated designs for bridges, waterfalls, streams, and plantings developed as gardenmaking emerged as an art form that would develop to its highest level in Japan's medieval age.

Early Japanese texts of the eleventh century, the Sakuteiki and the Senzui Narabini Yagyō no Zu, clearly describe techniques for building gardens. The authors recommend studying nature in order to understand aesthetic placement of garden elements. Different types of waterfalls, pond edgings, and islands are described, and auspicious and taboo rock arrangements detailed.

The texts link the beauty of nature to the art of gardening as a set of concepts that are still useful to garden designers today.

Techniques written down in the Sakuteiki can be seen in the famous Moss Temple, Saihō-ji, in the Western Hills of Kyoto. Said to have been designed by the great Buddhist priest Musō Soseki (1275-1351), the garden was originally built in traditional lake-and-islands pattern, but was infused with a new religious spirit, that of the Zen Buddhist sect, in 1339. Tamped-earth paths encircle the pond in the lower part of the 4½-acre space, designed as a stroll garden, in which views of the landscape change as one walks through its spaces. Earlier gardens were designed to be seen from the interior of a building or from a boat on a pond. Another and even more influential Musō innovation may be seen in the upper garden, built on a rocky hillside to the north. Here large, lichenous stones seem to tumble down the hillside in a series of waterfalls and stepped pools. Yet no water ever actually circulated here. Musō may have placed these stones as a powerful "dry landscape" composition, thought to be the first ever built for contemplation by the monks who inhabited the temple. The abstract power of this rock composition has influenced the designers of later *karesansui* gardens ever since.

Meditation Gardens

During the Muromachi period (1335-1573), small Zen gardens were built in sub-temples in which Zen priests tried many different approaches to the design of stone gardens. These gardens represented in three-dimensional form Zen discipline, philosophy, self-examination, and ultimate enlightenment. Often placed on the south-facing side of a Zen temple's prayer hall, these *karesansui* "meditation" gardens featured white sand or gravel as the ground cover, raked in various patterns to suggest waves, droplets, ripples, or other effects seen on a vast body of water such as a broad river or the sea.

Some of these gardens were more abstract than others. The famous garden of

Daisen-in, a subtemple of Kyoto's Daitoku-ji Temple complex, built in 1513, houses a miniature natural landscape said to be a three-dimensional representation of the Sung dynasty scroll paintings that influenced Zen thought of the time. Three sections of the garden, two of them less than ten feet in depth, hold stones arranged as a course of water falling over a waterfall, flowing through a mountain streambed, past a broad river and into a vast ocean, all indicated through stones and raked gravel. Perhaps the most famous Zen garden is Ryōan-ji, a raked gravel garden containing fifteen stones. Within a large, rectangular space the size of a tennis court, five "islands" of moss and stone, comprising five, two, three, two, and three rocks, respectively, rise from a bed of raked gravel symbolizing the sea. While the composition as a whole is asymmetrical, balance is achieved through hierarchy. One's eyes and mind travel around the garden in a kind of circle, from the highest rock to the lowest, giving the garden a sense of motion. From no point on the veranda can all fifteen rocks be seen at once; one rock is always hidden. Looking at the garden, one feels like the fifteenth rock, a part of the total composition. Soothed by the serene simplicity of the spare materials—gravel, rocks, and moss—one becomes an island, like Japan itself, floating upon a vast sea.

Karesansui, *or "dry landscape" gardens were built during the Muromachi period (1335 – 1573) in Zen Buddhist temples for the purpose of contemplation. Monks would meditate upon their white-gravelled, abstract stone compositions, as one means to attain a state of enlightenment.*

Eventually the oblong, white-gravelled space became too constricting for Zen designers. New techniques for creating the illusion of depth in a small space were developed. One was to use walls as a visual passage between the miniature landscape in the foreground and the larger landscape beyond. This technique, called *shakkei*, or "borrowed landscape," makes tiny gardens appear much larger. The foreground may be a dry landscape of rocks, moss and small shrubs, behind which lies a carefully groomed hedge, with a grove of trees behind it. The trees are pruned so that only the tops have branches, leaving long slim trunks that suggest a natural "frame." Enclosed by the hedge on the bottom, the trunks on the sides, and the branches above, the distant view, such as a mountain, becomes part of the garden. The eye travels between two

worlds, the miniature landscape in front, and the distant mountainscape in the background, to create a dynamic balance through depth.

The Momoyama period (1574-1603) brought two new aesthetic ideals to Japanese gardens. The first was a gorgeous, opulent look that the military dictator Toyotomi Hideyoshi demanded in his architecture and gardens. His Nishihonganji temple in southern Kyoto shows the effect of his "brilliant light" gardens, with an abundance of colorful, powerful rocks, often stolen from courtiers and vanquished foes. At the same time, a reaction to his extravagance set in, and the restraint, refinement, and dark simplicity of the tea ceremony became popular. Tea master Sen no Rikyū, Hideyoshi's aesthetic advisor, developed a style that infused gardens with a sense of impoverished elegance that influences gardenmaking even today.

Tea Gardens

The area that surrounds a tea house is called *roji*, literally, "dewy path," or tea garden. Its purpose is to spiritually prepare visitors by leading them on a journey of stepping stones, over thresholds, through gates, and past lanterns, to a water basin where they purify hands and mouth, before moving on to the teahouse, where the host serves powdered green tea in a ritualized ceremony.

Since a tea garden is designed to provide a series of spatial impressions in a tiny area, the design of its path is critical. Stepping stones (*tobiishi*) are a constant motif, variously used. Small *tobiishi* placed next to each other slow the pace and direct the gaze downward; larger stones enable the guest to stop to look at some special view; and long stone planks (*nobedan*) allow the step to quicken in anticipation of the tea house around the bend. Each stone has a purpose, whether it be to focus the visitor upon the act of moving through the garden, to rid the mind of mundane thoughts, or to anticipate the quiet serenity of the tea ceremony. Tea gardens, despite their tiny dimensions, often have multiple paths, closed or open to entry by the placement of a single

Three arched granite bridges link the Tortoise and the Crane islands to Tenshin-en's "mainland." A lichen-covered stone suggests the wing or the tail of a crane—a symbol of longevity and prosperity. Behind, on a distant shore, stands a stone lantern (ishidōrō) carved in the Kasuga style. Using a technique called shakkei, Tenshin-en's designer has "borrowed" the background landscape of The Fenway and made it part of the garden space.

Rooftiles (kawara) *are made of clay and have been baked four times, in order to withstand Boston's severe climate. A special emblem tile* (onigawara) *features the Museum's seal.*

reed-bound rock (*yogoseki*) upon the initial stepping stone in the path. Detours from the path are brief, perhaps only to wash one's hands in a stone basin. And always the path provides the continuity that links the various parts of the garden experience.

Current Trends in Japanese Gardening

Modern Japanese gardens, including Tenshin-en, often represent an amalgam of the three major styles of gardens: the stroll garden, the meditation garden, and the tea garden. Increasingly, Western and Chinese features are being incorporated into Japanese traditional design, in the form of public and semi-public parks, institutional gardens, and private residences.

Tenshin-en

Process and Project Team

The Museum of Fine Arts, Boston, asked an internationally known garden master from Kyoto, Professor Kinsaku Nakane, to design and construct a Japanese garden as an important addition to the Museum's world-renowned Asiatic collection. Funds for the project were donated by the Nippon Television Network Corporation, Chairman of the Board, Mr. Yōsōji Kobayashi.

As the garden master's project coordinator, my first responsibility was to assemble a project team to carry out Professor Nakane's design concept. I chose The Halvorson Company, a Boston landscape architecture firm and member of the American Society of Landscape Architects, to produce the technical documents and details necessary to build a garden of another culture in this country. Our mandate was to combine an acute sensitivity to the nuances of Japanese design with a full understanding of the legal and technical requirements of building in this country. Also included in the team were local subcontractors and craftsmen from Japan, each of whom brought specialized training to the different aspects of the project.

The garden evolved through collaboration, with each team member working in an atmosphere of trust and unstinting commitment to realize the master's concept. From Museum curatorial staff who guided the garden process and provided and conserved many of its artifacts, to the Italian masons who set Kyoto rooftiles on its walls; from the Japanese carpenters who built a traditional gate in Kyoto, dismantled it, and re-installed it on site, to the American carpenters who helped them, the master's concept was upheld by the efforts of every team member. The reward for the landscape team was a collaboration of the highest order.

A true Japanese garden derives from the landscape around it. Toward that end, the project team flew over New England in a small plane, exploring the region's rocky coastlines, deep forests, soft hillsides, and craggy mountains. The result is a garden that is an interpretation of two cultures, combining the depth of meaning of Japanese garden symbolism with a feeling of beauty and repose that comes from the New England landscape.

A dry waterfall suggests the scenery of vast mountains in a small space. Behind, stand Canadian hemlocks (Tsuga canadensis) and a stewartia tree (Stewartia pseudocamellia). Surrounding the waterfall are andromeda, azaleas, and ferns.

Professor Nakane, accompanied by his son and chief assistant, Shirō Nakane, was present to set the elements that made up the structure of the garden. To watch him was to see a true master at work. For six hot days in July 1987, Nakane set the rocks in the garden, like a conductor of a symphony orchestra. Attending to an image of power and beauty that existed only in his sketches and in his imagination, he set 178 stones.

With the aid of a 100-foot hydraulic crane, its intensely concentrating operator,

and three landscape crews, the shape of the garden began to emerge. Eight tractor-trailer truckloads of boulders, some weighing as much as eight tons, were chained to the crane's wire, one by one. Professor Nakane would indicate to one crew how far into the ground it should dig, and to another which way the stone should face; where its head, feet, front, and back should be. Watching every gesture he made, the crew placed the stones in the ground and made minute adjustments under Professor Nakane's watchful eye. (Professor Nakane speaks only Japanese, so all this was done without a word spoken.)

What was most remarkable was that Professor Nakane, in a calm and almost casual way, would set one stone at the *takiguchi* (waterfall), the next stone on the *tsurujima* (Crane Island), and the next in the foreground of the garden. He saw the whole in his mind's eye and worked around the garden to balance his composition right from the start. Each stone grouping had its internal dynamics and balance. When the composition was complete, nothing needed to be altered; the whole felt dynamic and yet balanced. His precision and his speed, not to mention his artistry, were wonderful to behold.

After he had set the stones, the walls and new sidewalks were installed. The following spring, Professor Nakane returned to complete the plantings. Called back due to a death at the Osaka University of the Arts, he set fifty-two trees on the day he arrived, and returned to Japan the next day. At that point, Shirō Nakane took over and set the remaining plantings, ornaments, and stepping stones, and supervised the erection of the Japanese gate.

Professor Nakane returned one more time, for the opening of the garden on October 24, 1988. At that time, he declined to speak, but chose instead to paint a sign for the garden in *sumie*, or Japanese ink. Inscribed is *ten*, *shin*, and *en* (with Chinese characters) in his own beautiful calligraphic hand. Since

Representing the Buddhist concept of shumisen or Mt. Sumeru—a mythic mountain around which the universe was thought to be centered—this dry waterfall appears to be the source for Tenshin-en's sea. Set in a triangle around a "waterfall stone," rounded washed river stones complete the illusion of water falling in tiers into the white gravel sea.

then, Tenshin-en has been open to the public from spring through fall and is viewed with delight by thousands of people every year.

Design Features of Tenshin-en

Tenshin-en is designed as a viewing garden in the *karesansui*, or dry landscape garden, style, harkening back to Zen temple gardens of the fifteenth century in Japan. Water is suggested by the raked gravel "sea" that unites the landforms of the garden: the mountains, islands, and rocky shoreline formed by mounded earth and rocks.

Using the *shakkei* technique of borrowed landscape, curved shorelines and bridges within the garden echo the Olmsted-designed Fenway landscape that abuts the Museum on its north side. Frederick Law Olmsted, America's premier garden master, designed parks and green spaces during the late 1800s, creating Boston's "Emerald Necklace," linking open space from Franklin Park to the Boston Common in one nearly continuous sweep of green. Although Olmsted conceived and designed on a scale far vaster than Tenshin-en's miniature landscape, he understood a similar need to evoke a harmonious understanding of nature. In 1879 he wrote: "We want a ground to which people may easily go after their day's work is done, and where they may stroll for an hour, seeing, hearing, and feeling nothing of the bustle and jar of the streets, where they shall, in effect, find the city put far away from them."

Symbolism

An understanding of its symbolism augments one's appreciation of the garden. The dry "waterfall" to the back and left of the garden (see D on the plan, page 46) represents the Buddhist concept of *shumisen,* or Mt. Sumeru, a mythic mountain that was thought to support the heavens above and the world below, around which the universe was thought to be centered. The two "islands" in the left and right center of the garden (E, F) are two of the "Mystic Isles of the Immortals," mythical Taoist islands that were said to bring immortality and prosperity to those who incorporated them in their gardens. To the left is the Tortoise Island (*kamejima*), and to the right the Crane Island (*tsurujima*). According to an old Chinese saying, "The Crane lives a thousand, the Tortoise ten thousand years." Looking carefully, one can see the head, feet, tail, and flippers of the Tortoise, and the head, wings, and tail of the Crane.

"The idea behind this landscape," says Professor Nakane, "is the re-creation of the essence of mountains, the ocean and islands in a garden setting, as I have seen them in the beautiful landscape of New England. The mountains and islands symbolize the natural beauty of this region, and, at the same time, mean enduring prosperity and happiness for the Museum visitors." Some of Professor Nakane's imagery suggests itself in the garden's design features. The rocky coastline to the right reminds the viewer of the Maine coast, and the two large rocks in the Crane Island suggest Mt. Fuji on the right, and one of New England's best-known peaks, Mt. Monadnock, on the left. Looking carefully, one can see a profile much like that of the "Old Man in the Mountain" on the floating island between the Crane Island and the rocky coast. The stepping stone path area is an abstraction of deep forests, and the mossy hillside behind the Crane Island reminds us of the softly forested landscape of New England.

The Stones

The garden is approximately 10,000 square feet, or about one-quarter of an acre. In it are 178 rocks from Topsfield, Boxford, and Rockport, weighing a total of about 400 tons. These are set according to ancient rules and traditions, dating back to Japan's Middle Ages. A dark granite vertical stone and base, carved in Japan, is located to the left of the waterfall. It says "Ten-shin-en" in Chinese characters taken from documents in Okakura's own handwriting, a gift of the garden's donor, Mr. Yōsōji Kobayashi.

Stepping stones (tobiishi) *are carefully placed to lead the visitor on a journey along a roji— a "dewy path." Rules for setting stepping stones are simple: place each stone one fist's length apart from the next, raise stones at least one-half to one inch above the surface of the ground, and make sure that each rock's shape complements the next, to create a harmonious, meandering voyage through space.*

The Wall and Japanese Gate

The wall is a modern interpretation of a Japanese mud-and-wattle wall (*tsujibei*), seen in temple compounds and surrounding traditional gardens all over Japan. This wall, varying in height from five to seven feet, was constructed of poured concrete mixed with a light colorant, which was then sandblasted to roughen the texture. The base band is made of granite from Deer Isle, Maine, like the façade of the West Wing, to provide the sense of a traditional foundation upon which the wall rests.

Atop the wall, visible from the outside, is a cap of simple rooftiles (*kawara*), designed to meld with the spare lines of the West Wing. From the inside, one sees the "roof" of the wall, which is covered in rooftiles imported from Kyoto. These are made of clay, baked four times rather than the usual two, to accommodate Boston's severe climate. Yokoyama Seiga Kōjō, an old Kyoto firm which specializes in shrine and temple rooftiles, supplied the 1500 pieces that make up the roof. There are round rooftiles (*marugawara*), stacked tiles (*noshigawara*), beam tiles (*sangawara*), and eaves tiles (*nokigawara*). A special emblem tile (*onigawara*), which features the Museum's seal, was also made up and grouted to the end wall at the school group entrance.

The gate (*kabukemon*, or "hanging gate") is a traditional, medieval-style gate used in Japan for mountain castles or large palaces. It was chosen, in part, as a Japanese-style horizontal counterpoint to I.M. Pei's large concrete

A Japanese maple (Acer palmatum) *veils a stone lantern* (ishidōrō) *and Japanese cypress gate. This* kabukemon *or "hanging gate" was constructed in Japan, disassembled, and then flown to Boston, where traditional carpenters reassembled it.*

beam at the entrance to the Museum's West Wing. The gate is built of Japanese cypress, a wood with excellent natural preservatives. Special design features of the gate are the thirteen-inch-wide post and beams, the *kasugi*, or "umbrella wood" curved beams above the two small doors, the ornamental nail covers and ironwork.

The gate was constructed in Japan by Suzuki Kōmuten, carpenters (*miya daiku*) who specialize in traditional Japanese structures. After being erected for approval in Japan, it was disassembled and rebuilt in Boston. The wrought iron fittings, hinges, and nail covers were fabricated in Japan, and are of traditional design. The small decorative nail covers are called *kazari kugi*; the large round ones are called either *manjūkanamono* for the Japanese candy of the same name, or *chichikanamono*, "breast ironwork."

The copper-roofed information board is constructed of Japanese cypress, and holds a panel that tells the name of the garden, its history, and information regarding its use. Similar structures can be found in front of most temple buildings in Japan.

The Water Basin

The water basin or *chōzubachi*, enables the visitor to ritually purify the body and mind in preparation for contemplating the garden and for receiving inspiration and renewal from its spiritual meaning. Similar stone basins were used in tea gardens as vessels for ritual cleansing before taking tea. This *chōzubachi* is of the *fusen* style (*fu* means "to proclaim" and *sen* means "spring of water").

The stones around the water basin are arranged in the original Kohō-an style. The large stepping stone upon which one kneels to partake of the water is called a *maeishi* or "front stone." The stone to its right is the *yūokeishi* or "hot water container stone" on which such a container would be placed in winter

This water basin (chōzubachi) *is of the* fusen *style. The Chinese character on the left* (fu) *means "to proclaim," and the character on the right* (sen) *means "spring of water."*

This Japanese lantern of the Edo period (1603 – 1867) was originally located in the Japanese courtyard garden in the Asiatic galleries. It is located just behind the water basin, so that it can cast light over that area at night.

so that guests could add hot water to the basin to warm their hands. The stone to the left is the *teshokuishi* or "hand candle stone" on which a portable candlestick might be placed if using the garden at night.

The Stone Lanterns

Stone lanterns were originally votive lights placed in front of Buddhist temple buildings. In later years they were designed specifically for garden use, to light the path to a tea house, or to illuminate certain areas of a garden. The small Japanese lantern of the Edo period (1603-1867) was originally in the Japanese court of the Asiatic collection. It has a tall mushroom-shaped "hat" and is placed so that it can cast light over the water basin at night.

The *kasuga*-style lantern , of the tall, votive light style, is a reproduction of one from the Kawageta Temple, considered a "Very Important Cultural Property" by the Japanese Government. The original lantern was made in 1311 and is a very good example of late Kamakura period (1185-1333) lanterns. It shows the prevailing concern with power and beauty in its "attacking lion" and peacock carvings on the lantern. Single lotus petals are carved at the base, a Buddhist symbol of the soul's ascent from mud to the glory of flowering. The top curving roof is designed in the form of *warabite*, or edible fern.

Another *kasuga*-style lantern is a reproduction of the main lantern at the Jōruri-ji Temple near Kyoto, carved about 1366. The shape of this lantern follows the composition of the Kawageta lantern, but is narrower throughout. The lotus petals are taller, the window smaller, and there is a steeper curve to the roof.

The large, sixteenth-century–style Korean lantern of the Chosŏn period was originally located in the Museum's courtyard. The roof and the base are of different origins. The lantern located outside the garden wall, next to the information board, is a Meiji period lantern, dating to about 1880, and fea-

This Kasuga-style lantern stands amid the soft curves of azaleas, mountain laurel, and iris. The groundcover moss, known as haircap moss (Polytrichum commune), is commonly found in open woodlands of acid soils and dappled sunlight. Like its Japanese counterpart — sugigoke — it looks like miniature cryptomeria trees and is soft and verdant when supplied with sufficient moisture.

This nanako-gaki, *or "twill weave" fence is the simplest form of bamboo enclosure. It is used more in public parks than in gardens, as a subtle barrier. Made of shaved pieces of bamboo that are curved and inserted into the ground, this* nanako-gaki *keeps people on Tenshin-en's curved path.*

features ornamental friezes of mountains and deer, with lotus leaves as decoration around its base, donated to the garden by Mr. and Mrs. Leonard Rosner.

The Paths

Several kinds of paths define the circulation through Tenshin-en. The path outside the wall to the garden gate (B) is of hewn granite called *shikiishi,* or "cut stones." The entry path is a *nobedan,* or "plank stone" path, much like traditional interior garden paths, but widened to accommodate wheelchairs and strollers. All granite used in the garden is from Deer Isle, Maine. The cut stepping stones are surrounded by black washed Mexican river stones set in mortar. The curved path leads to the *shikiishi,* the "cut stone" terrace on which are three *shōgi* benches of traditional design. Stepping stones paths called *tobiishi* take the visitor to the Korean lantern, the water basin, or as an alternate route back to the gate. In this way the garden embodies the principle of *shin-gyō-sō*: the path outside the gate is of the *shin,* or "formal" style, the stepping stones are of the *sō* or "informal" style, and the curved *nobedan* path is of the *gyō* style—somewhere between informal and formal in style.

Three bridges (G) link the "islands" with the "mainland" and form a path taking the viewer on a visual, rather than an actual journey. The longest of these *soribashi* or "curved bridges" is seventeen feet long and weighs 1.5 tons.

The Plantings

More than seventy plant species give color and texture to the garden. Cherries (*sakura*), Japanese maples (*momiji* or *kaede*) and pines (*matsu*) are all signature plants of a Japanese garden, and serve as symbols of the changing seasons. Azaleas of many colors and varieties provide continuous bloom from spring into summer and combine with haircap moss (*Polytrichum commune*) to create a soft and verdant groundcover. A mixture of Japanese and American species serves to create a new horticultural interpretation of an ancient art form.

Trees

Japanese maples are signature plants of a Japanese garden. Used to create a feeling of mountain scenery at the edge of a forest, they link open land to woodland. Broadleafed evergreen trees are scarce in the Northeast, so American hollies (*Ilex opaca*), were used in place of some of the evergreen oaks that act as tall evergreen screens in Japan, and give the sense of a deep forest. Needleleaf trees, including compact selections of Canadian hemlocks (*Tsuga canadensis*) and cryptomeria (*Cryptomeria japonica* 'Yoshino') are used to create a lush background to the waterfall and mountain path areas. Cryptomeria (*sugi*) were part of the indigenous vegetation in Japan and are planted extensively in holy areas such as shrine precincts. Red pines (*Pinus densiflora*) and Tanyoso pines (*Pinus densiflora* 'Umbraculifera') are used to highlight the islands.

Deciduous trees used in the garden include *Stewartia pseudocamellia*, mountain ash (*Sorbus decora*), star magnolia (*Magnolia stellata*), and of course, cherries: the weeping cherry by the gate (*Prunus subhirtella var. pendula*), the October cherries (*Prunus subhirtella var.* 'Autumnalis') and Sargent's cherries (*Prunus sargentii*). Cherries are beloved by the Japanese as symbols of a life well-lived: they bloom suddenly and abundantly, but are gone nearly overnight, suggesting a good way to face death.

Shrubs

The 1100 shrubs in the garden give it its finished, full, and colorful look. Five hundred azaleas of many varieties provide color and bloom over two months in the spring. Early bloomers include the Korean azalea (*Azalea poukhanensis*) and varieties of *R. mucronulatum*. The popular 'Delaware Valley White' azaleas and early reds ('A. hinocrimson and hinodegiri') are mixed with mid-bloomers of various colors: salmon ('Guy Yerkes'), silver-pink ('Kaempo'), white with pink throat ('Geisha'), white ('Girard's Pleasant White', 'Polar Bear'), rose-red ('Vyking'), and the beautiful 'Purple Gem' rhododendron.

The foreground rock composition suggests the "flipper" of a giant tortoise, a symbol of longevity and prosperity. On its "back" grows a tabletop pine (Pinus densiflora Umbraculifera), *pink and red azaleas, andromedas* (Pieris japonica), *and verdant spears of iris* (Iris siberica). *Behind, a seven-tiered pagoda* (ishidō) *from the Museum collection points to the sky.*

Late-blooming varieties include the North Tisbury hybrids, 'Wintergreen', 'Yuka', and 'Marilee'. Azaleas are pruned in the *karikomi*, or cloud-form shape, to suggest the billowing forms of hills and to soften the base of the stones.

Other shrubs used extensively are mountain laurels (*Kalmia latifolia*), andromeda (*Pieris japonica, P. floribunda*), enkianthus (*Enkianthus campanulatus*), kerria (*Kerria japonica*), daphne (*Daphne burkwoodi* 'Carol Mackie'), forsythia (*Forsythia intermedia* 'Arnold Dwarf'), barberries (*Berberis thunbergii, B. mentorensis*), junipers (*Juniperus procumbens* 'Nana', *J. chinesis* 'Sargenti'), euonymus (*Euonymus alatus*), holly (*Ilex pendunculosa*), and dwarf spiraea (*Spirea japonica* 'Little Princess').

Perennials and Groundcovers

Six hundred perennials adorn the garden. Hostas and liriope are used along with ferns of many varieties to soften the rocks; leatherwood, lady, hart's tongue, Japanese painted, Christmas, and maidenhair ferns abound in the garden. Hostas include 'Gold Standard', 'Green Fountain', 'Francee', 'Blue Cadet', 'Nakiana', and 'Flavo Circinalis'; the five giant hostas outside the walls are 'Halcyon', 'Christmas Tree', 'Nigrescens', 'Frances Williams', and 'Blue Angel'.

Other perennials include bloodroot (*Sanguinaria canadensis*), trillium (*Trillium grandiflorum*), goatsbeard (*Aruncus korean*), lady's mantle (*Alchemilla pubescens*), iris (*Iris ensata, I. sibirica,* and *I. cristata*), geraniums (*Geranium endressi* 'Johnson's Blue', *G. sanguineum*), astilbes (*astilbe chinesis* 'Pumila', A. 'William Buchanan'), bleeding heart (*Dicentra eximia* 'Zestful'), ginger (*Asarum european*), and liriopes and sedges (*Liriope spicata, Carex conica variegata*). One can also spot pachysandra (*P. terminalis* 'Cutleaf') planted as a specimen near the water basin and stepping stone path. The groundcover moss is *Polytrichum commune*, known as haircap moss (see sidebar on the care and cultivation of haircap moss).

Hosta ('Golden Showers') *thrives among a stand of enkianthus* (Enkianthus campanulatus) *and fringed bleeding heart* (Dicentra eximia) *whose rose-colored blossoms and fern-like foliage contrast with the softness of the haircap moss.*

Carved in Japan, this handsome granite stone with base is located to the left of the waterfall. It says "Ten-shin-en" in Chinese characters, copied from documents in Okakura's own handwriting. It is a gift from the garden's donor, Mr. Yōsōji Kobayashi.

Tenshin-en is open to Museum visitors from late spring through early fall, Tuesdays through Sundays. It may always be viewed from the windows of the North Gallery on the second floor.

Julie Moir Messervy, project coordinator for Tenshin-en and designer of the Linda J. Davison Memorial Path at the Arnold Arboretum in Boston, is a landscape designer living in Wellesley, Massachusetts. She is the author of *Contemplative Gardens* (Howell Press, 1990) and is currently finishing a new book *The Inward Garden* to be published by Little, Brown in early 1994.

Tenshin-en's designer aimed to meld the landscape of the New England region with elements and symbolism from traditional Japanese gardens. Here, the visitor gets a sense of New England's beautiful coastline, with its mossy promontories and harbors, and its backdrop of azaleas, kerria, andromedas, and mountain laurel — a true marriage of North American and Japanese plantings.

Maintenance

Contrary to popular opinion, a Japanese garden is not a low-maintenance landscape. One day a week, every week during the garden's open season, a maintenance crew comes to take care of the garden. Every week the crew prunes certain trees and shrubs, weeds the moss, and rakes the gravel. Other activities occur at specific intervals throughout the year: moss is cut for propagation, perennials are cut back or divided, fertilizers or horticultural sprays are applied, hemlock bark mulch is spread, and azaleas are deadheaded and pruned at least twice a year to maintain their shape and size.

Visitors are always curious about the manner in which the garden is raked. Crushed granite gravel from Mt. Airy, North Carolina, represents the "sea" of the garden's landscape. A heavy, eight-tine rake is used to give the effect of ripples on the water's surface. Starting from the near, right-hand corner of the garden, the crew rakes in lines parallel with the West Wing wall. When the raker reaches an obstacle, such as a stone or island, he stands on it and rakes around it in a circle, continuing the pattern under the bridges and around all detached stones. Finally, the raker follows the edge of the garden's "sea" around the perimeter until meeting the gate. The abstract lines of "water" are most apparent during rainy or cloudy days, or when the textures are emphasized by a thin veneer of snow.

Each year, thousands of visitors come to Tenshin-en to learn about another culture's garden art, to enjoy the verdant atmosphere, or to seek a moment's peace. Please visit Tenshin-en and sit quietly on its benches, stroll along its paths, or view it from the West Wing windows. For in the Garden of the Heart of Heaven, you will feel the truth of the words of Okakura Tenshin, the garden's namesake, who once said, "One may be in the midst of a city, and yet feel as if one were far away from the dust and din of civilization."

The Cultivation and Care of Haircap Moss

Soft mosses carpeting a hillside suggest the special, secret places of chidhood. How ironic, then, that so much time and effort is spent trying to eradicate them. As the Garden of the Heart of Heaven shows, with appropriate care, mosses can be cultivated in your own backyard.

At Tenshin-en, its haircap moss (*Polytrichum commune*) looks just like the Japanese version called *sugigoke*, or cryptomeria moss. It adapts to a variety of conditions ranging from semi-shade to full sun. Thriving in acid soils and plentiful moisture, moss can be transplanted as sod if one is lucky enough to find it. Although moss sods can be purchased much like turf in Japan, I know of no nursery in New England that propagates moss and sells it. The usual local source, then, is from colonies of moss growing in the wild, where you should take only what you need and leave the rest undisturbed so that more may grow again in the future. Notice the conditions under which it grows in nature and reproduce those as closely as possible on your site.

First, prepare your soil by removing all existing lawn grass and perennial plantings from the new bed. Then dig your moss in thick clumps that include several inches of soil under each square of moss, and transfer it quickly to the new bed. Place it and tamp it in, using your fist to remove all air pockets that could dry out the rhizoids that anchor the sod. Water it well and continue irrigating when needed. I suggest to my clients that they install an irrigation system and mist the moss at least once a day, especially during the dry summer months.

Moss dislikes fertile soil, and will die if you apply any sort of fertilizer to it. At Tenshin-en, we fertilize adjacent plantings with a probe, never by hand. Moss from the wild needs frequent weeding in the first years, and raking or vacuuming in the fall when leaves fall on it.

In the early spring, we regenerate mosses in sparse areas by giving the longer

"hairs" a trimming. We gather these pieces and dry them on a widowsill for several days until they become powder, then spread them over prepared areas. Spores from adjacent moss sporeheads are released and settle on the dried, powdery cuttings. Other methods that are though to accomplish the same purpose include making "moss milkshakes" in a blender, and applying buttermilk or aluminum sulfate to the areas in which you hope to grow your moss.

There are said to be 14,000 varieties of this beautiful and underused groundcover, creating a lush, verdant carpet in the garden, setting off both our craggy New England rocks, and our delicate ferns, lichens, and wildflowers, the velvety moss touches deep into our soul.

Reference: See the section on moss gardens by Michael B. Trimble in "Japanese Gardens," from *Plants and Gardens, the Brooklyn Botanic Garden Record* 41, no 3, (autumn 1985).

TENSHIN-EN
The Garden of the Heart of Heaven

天心園

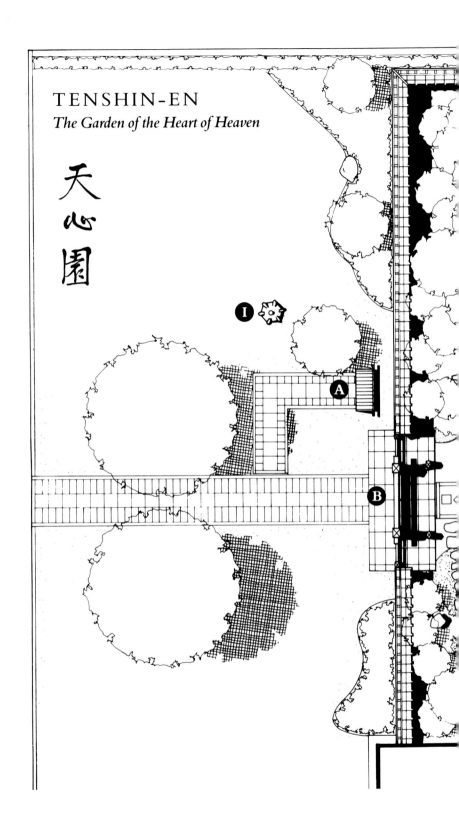

KEY

A Information Board

B Gate

C Terrace

D Mt. Sumeru with dry waterfall

E Tortoise Island

F Crane Island

G Bridges

H Water basin

I Lanterns

J Pagoda

K North Gallery

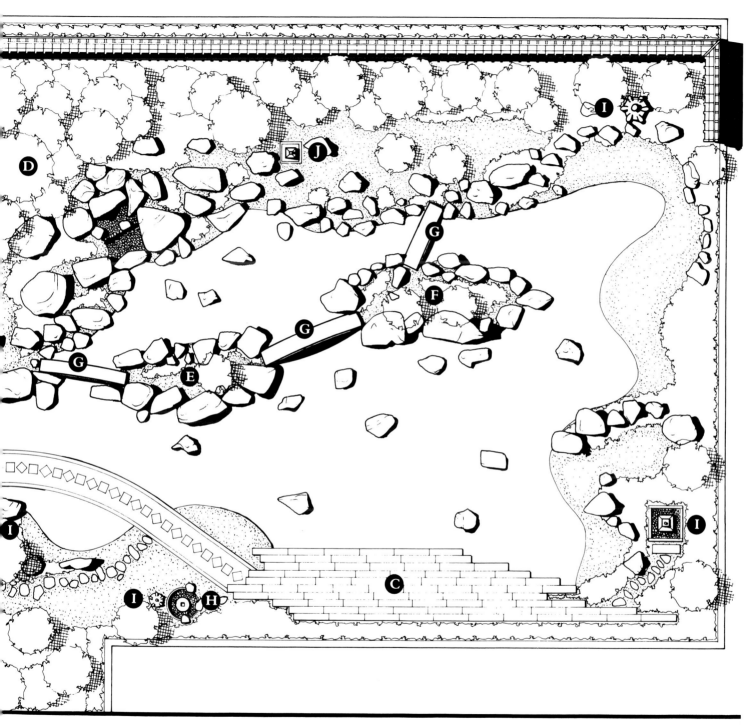